**COPTIC ORTHODOX
PATRIARCHATE**

See of St. Mark

*Contemplations
On the Prayer of the Holy Week*

THINE IS THE POWER
AND THE GLORY

**BY
H.H. POPE SHENOUDA III**

Title	: Thine is the Power and the Glory.
Author	: H. H. Pope Shenouda III.
Translated By	: St. Mark Coptic Orthodox Church, Los Angeles.
Revised By	: Mrs. Wedad Abbas.
Illustrated By	: Sister Sawsan.
Edition	: The second April 1992.
Typesetting	: J.C. Center, Heliopolis.
Printing	: Dar El Tebaa El Kawmia, Cairo.
Reprinted	: St Shenouda Monastery, Sydney Australia, March 2017
Legal Deposit No.	: 3 6 5 4 /1992.
Revised	: COEPA -1997

H.H. Pope Shenouda III
117th Pope and Patriarch of Alexandria
and the See of St Mark

CONTENTS

THE IMPORTANCE OF
THE PASSION WEEK

The Passion Week or the Holy Pascha (Passover) is the most important period in the year and the richest spiritually. It is a week full of Holy memories of the most crucial stage of salvation and the outstanding chapter in the story of redemption.

The Church chose for this week certain readings from both the Old and the New Testaments, which reflect, the most passionate feelings that explain God's relation with Man. The Church also chose some deep hymns and spiritual contemplation to suit the occasion.

In the early Church, our Saintly Fathers used to receive this week with respect and reverence, and act in great humility.

While fasting, they abstained from eating any sweet food like honey or jam, as they considered it not appropriate to taste any sweet thing while commemorating the Lord's suffering for them. Some used not to cook anything during that week, as a matter of devotion, and lest cooking should distract them from worshipping. The majority of Christians used to eat nothing but bread and salt. Those who were physically capable abstained from Friday night till Easter Sunday.

As a sign of devotion during this week, women used not to put make up or wear jewellery. People devoted all their time for worshipping; they gathered in Churches for prayer and contemplation.

The Great Emperor Theodosius was one of the Christian Kings and Rulers who ordered all Government Houses and Business to cease work, to enable people to concentrate on worshipping. Prisoners were also allowed to go to Church and join in the ceremonies of this Great Week, hoping that it would help them to reform. Christian masters also used to relieve their slaves from work all the Pascha Week to enable them to worship the Lord like their masters, without any discrimination. So both masters and slaves were able to worship God and enjoy the effectiveness and depth of this week.

The Passion Week's Rite:

During this week, the Holy Church concentrates on one subject: The Lord Christ's suffering. For this reason, the Psalm readings and the Canonical Hours which cover various subjects relating to the Lord Jesus Christ including His birth, His ministry, His Resurrection, Ascension and sitting on the Father's right hand and His Second Coming in His Glory, are replaced by a special hymn chosen by the Church especially for the Pascha Week in which we address the Lord suffering for us saying:

✤ *"Thine is the Power, the Glory, the Blessing and the Honour, forever Amen, Emmanuel our   God and King* "
✤ *"Thine is the Power, the Glory, the Blessing and the Honour, forever Amen,   Our Lord   Jesus Christ"*,
✤ *"Thine is the Power, the Glory, the Blessing and the Honour, forever Amen ..."* adding to it .. ***"Our Good***

Saviour" from Wednesday night, as the plot to betray the Lord Christ was the practical step towards salvation.

This prayer, is repeated ten times every day.; five during daytime and five at night, ie. during the following hours: First, Third, Sixth, Ninth and Eleventh.

In each of these prayers, we turn to our God and Saviour in His passions and say, "we know who You are, for "Thine is the Power, Glory, Blessing and Honour, forever Amen."

With this prayer, we follow the Lord Christ step by step along the incidents of this week that preceded the crucifixion. What then are these incidents? And how does the Church act during this week?

How did The Suffering Start?

On Palm Sunday, the Lord Jesus Christ went to Jerusalem where He was gloriously received as a King: The people praised and cheered Him with palms, spreading their robes under His feet, and the whole city was in turmoil *(Matt. 21:10)*. This annoyed the chief priests and the elders of the people: scribes, Pharisees and Sadducees.

They envied Him for the great love people felt for Him, so they started thinking of a way to get rid of Him! They were more upset when He entered the temple and expelled all who were buying and selling. They then asked Him, *"By what authority are You doing these things?" (Matt.21:23)*. Since then they decided to kill Him, telling one another *"Look, the world has gone after Him," (John. 12:19)*.

The chiefs' desire to kill the Lord Christ was due to their envy, but the puzzling thing is the change in the multitude's attitude; they received Him like a King, then shouted to Pilate, *"Crucify Him, crucify Him! " (Luke. 23:21).*

When the crowds cheered Jesus, they looked at Him as an earthly King, *"Blessed is He who comes in the name of the LORD! Blessed is the kingdom of our father David" (Mark 11:9-10).* But the Lord Jesus refused a Kingdom on earth, as His is a Heavenly Spiritual one. The plot to get rid of the Nazarene was then a natural reaction from the Chiefs who lost hope in the long awaited kingdom!!

The church considers the end of Palm Sunday Mass the beginning of the Passion Week, as the plot to kill the Lord Jesus Christ started to develop since then.

During this week the Church's Icons, Pillars and Lectern and sometimes even the walls are all covered with black cloth, creating an atmosphere of mourning. It makes everyone feel that he is sharing in the Lord's sufferings, as said by St. Paul, *"that I may know Him and the power of His Resurrection and the fellowship of His sufferings". (Phil. 3:10).*

General Prayer For the Departed:

Through the Passion Week, the Church is preoccupied with the Lord's sufferings only, there is no raising of incense even for funerals, but replaced by the Pascha prayers and readings.

For this reason, a general prayer for the departed is held after Palm Sunday Mass, for the souls of those who pass away during the Holy Pascha. The priest prays on some water for this purpose, and not for blessing the palms as some may think.

During these prayers we have to confess our sins to the Lord in true repentance, as we never know when our life will end...

After this funeral mass and the dismissing of the congregation, prayers are carried forth outside the camp.

Outside the Camp:

Under the Law of the Old Testament, sin offering was to be burnt outside the camp *(Lev. 4:12,21),* so it would not. defile the camp with the congregation's sins.

Thus the Lord Christ who took away the sins of the whole world, suffered outside the Holy City. They considered Him a sinner, sent Him outside the Camp and crucified Him. St. Paul explained, and referred to this matter by saying:

"Let us go forth therefore to Him outside the camp, bearing His reproach." (Heb. 13:13).

The Holy Church follows the Lord's steps during the Pascha Week and goes with Him outside the camp, closing the veil. The Church also leaves the first Chancel, the Chancel of Saints, and moves the Lectern to the second Chancel to pray away from the Altar, outside the Sanctuary and the camp, bearing His reproach and saying:

"Thine is the Power, the Glory, the Blessing and the Honour, forever Amen... "

With this hymn, we follow the Lord Jesus Christ in His passion, step by step, contemplating on every word we say to Him in His Passion...

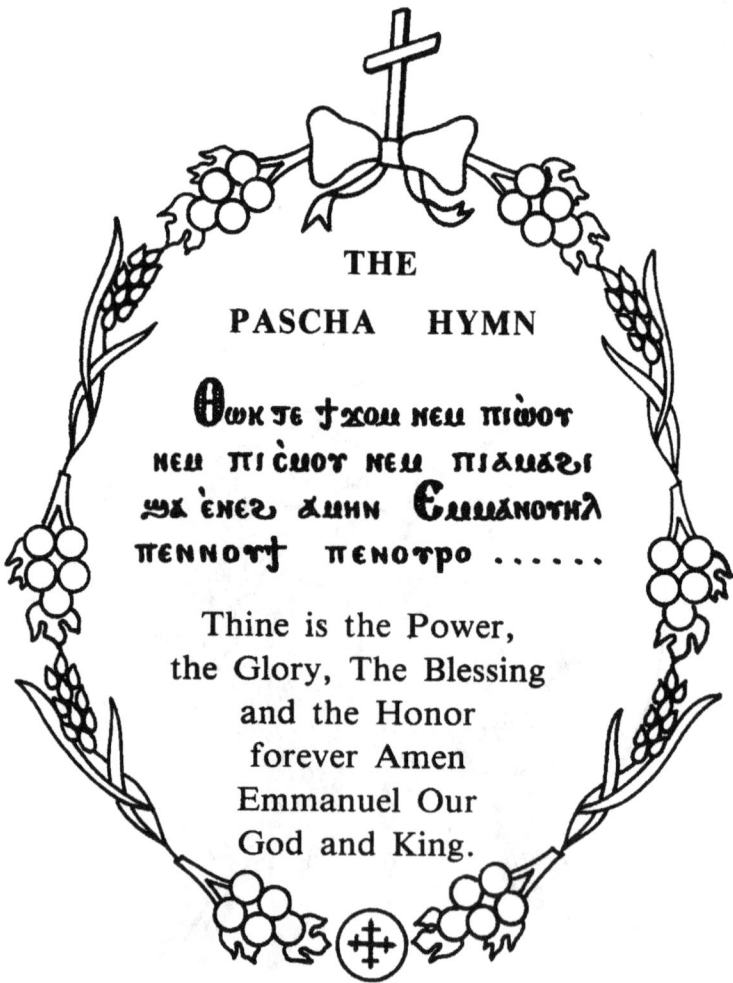

THE
PASCHA HYMN

Ⲑⲱⲕ ⲧⲉ ϯϫⲟⲙ ⲛⲉⲙ ⲡⲓⲱ̀ⲟⲩ
ⲛⲉⲙ ⲡⲓⲥ̀ⲙⲟⲩ ⲛⲉⲙ ⲡⲓⲁⲙⲁϩⲓ
ϣⲁ ⲉ̀ⲛⲉϩ ⲁⲙⲏⲛ Ⲉⲙⲙⲁⲛⲟⲩⲏⲗ
ⲡⲉⲛⲛⲟⲩϯ ⲡⲉⲛⲟⲩⲣⲟ ......

Thine is the Power,
the Glory, The Blessing
and the Honor
forever Amen
Emmanuel Our
God and King.

13

THE PASCHA HYMN

Thine is the Power, the Glory, the Blessing and the Honour, forever Amen...

We sing this hymn for the Lord Christ all through the Passion Week, following all His movements. We sing it instead of the Canonical Hours, the five day prayers and the five night prayers. We repeat the hymn twelve times in each prayer instead of the twelve psalms that are included in each prayer of the Canonical Hours.

The Lord Christ left Jerusalem to Bethany, were we follow Him saying, *"Thine is the Power, the Glory, the Blessing and the Honour"*... The Chief priests were annoyed when the Lord cleared the temple, and said, "By what authority are You doing these things?" But we say, *"Thine is the Power, the Glory, the Blessing and the Honour... Emmanuel our God and King"*... They planned to kill Him while we defend Him saying, *"Thine is the Power, the Glory, the Blessing and the Honour... forever Amen"*...

The Lord, in humility, bent to wash the disciples' feet, and we praise Him saying "Thine is the Power, the Glory, the Blessing and the Honor"... The Lord was praying at Gethsemane in such agony that His sweat was like drops of blood and we proclaim, "Thine is the Power and the Glory"...

We follow Him hour by hour; when arrested, put under trial in the presence of His enemies, crowned with thorns, flogged, falling under the Cross, nailed, till He commanded His Spirit into the hands of the Father and when He took the robber on His right with Him into Paradise, and we sing to Him all the time the hymn, "*Thine is the Power, the Glory, the Blessing and the Honour...forever Amen.*

THINE IS THE POWER
Ѳⲱⲕ ⲧⲉ ϯϫⲟⲙ

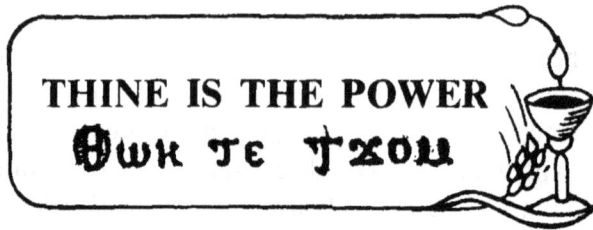

The first thing we praise the Lord Jesus Christ for, during the Passion Week, is His Power. Yes, Lord, Thine is the power as... St. Paul said, *"Christ the Power of God. " (1 Cor. 1:24).*

It is true, Lord, that some might think You were weak on the Cross, but we know who You are. The first thing we know about Your Power is that You are the Creator. *"All things were made through Him, and without Him nothing was made that was made"(John. 1:3).* You have the power too as a Judge who will come in glory to judge both the living and the dead.

Indeed, this crucified Lord who seemed to the people then weak, had they considered what He had done throughout all the days He spent among them, they would have known how powerful He had been in everything.

He was Powerful in His Miracles and His Holiness:

0 Lord, You alone of all the powerful, defeated the sin, the world and the devil, while all the others were too weak to resist sin, *For she has cast down many wounded, And all who were slain by her were strong men" (Prov. 7:26)* As it is said in the Holy Bible, *"They have all turned aside, They have together become corrupt; There is none who does good, No,* not one" *(Ps. 14:3)*. But You God, You are the Only One who challenged the whole world, saying, *"Which of you convicts Me of sin". (John. 8:46)*.

You are the only One who overcame the Devil and said, *"for the ruler of this world is coming, and he has nothing in Me" (John. 14:30)*. In the Revelation, they sang for You, *"For You alone are Holy,". (Rev. 15:4)*. You alone are powerful in Your Holiness, *"Holy, harmless, undefiled, separate from sinners, and has become higher than the heavens" (Heb. 7:26)*.

Lord, Your miracles proved Your wonderful Power, as You... " *had done among them the works which no one else did" (John. 15:24)*.

Your Power over Nature was shown: when You rebuked the wind and the waves and when You walked on the water. David sang for You saying, *"You rule the raging of the sea: when its waves rise, You still them" (Ps. 89:9)*. Thine is the Power, Lord...

You showed Your Power over sickness and death: as you healed all diseases and weaknesses of the people, especially the incurable ones. You opened the eyes of the blind, cleansed those with leprosy, healed the woman suffering from haemorrhages, the 38 years paralytic, the paralysed who was lowered down through the roof and the man with the withered hand.

Lord, You raised the dead, even that who had been in the tomb for four days and there was stench...

You showed Your Power as a Creator: when You fed thousands with 5 loaves and 2 fish. You even created a new substance when you turned the water into wine and when you made eyes for the man who was born blind.

Your Power over the devils was shown by casting away evil spirits, who left many saying, " *You are the Son of God."* You rebuked the demons and did not let them speak.

Your miracles are countless, Lord, as John the Beloved said, *"And there are also many other things that Jesus did, which if they were written one by one, I suppose that even the world itself could not contain the books that would be written" (John. 21:25).*

Beside all these aspects of the Lord's Power, the puzzling one is shown in His suffering and crucifixion where He gives us a new concept of the meaning of Power.

What is this new concept of power?

The Lord's New Concept of Power:

The world's concept of Power differs from that introduced by the Lord Jesus Christ.
To the World, it means violence and the ability to strike, to defend oneself and to subject others.

The Lord set an example of the Power which loves and sacrifices, endures and gives without limits.

When we think of Power, we have to look at it from the spiritual side, not the physical. That is how we should look at the Lord Christ in His sufferings.

The materialistic world, poor indeed, thinks that the Lord Christ was weak when they struck Him on the face, mocked Him and crucified Him. That would have been true if the Lord Christ had those insults due to His inability, but in fact, He was far more powerful than all those who struck, mocked and crucified Him.

He had the power to destroy them all, but He did no because He loved them and His love was more powerful than death. He was able to put them to death but He did not because He came to save them from death and by His own death to give life.

We glorify the Lord's endurance, which convinces us that Power is in endurance, as the apostle says, *"We then who are strong ought to bear with the scruples of the weak, and not to please ourselves" (Rom. 15:1)*.

Some people are too weak to endure; even the least insult provokes them and makes them lose control and turn to revenge. It shows their weakness and lack of power of endurance.

The Lord Christ was powerful in His endurance, and this demonstrates the power of His love. For a person who has love is able to endure, while failure to endure shows lack of love.

The Lord Christ came to take away our sins, "*all we like sheep have gone astray; we have turned everyone to his own way,. and the Lord has laid on Him the iniquity of us all*" *(Is. 53:6).* The Lord sacrificed Himself for our sins and for our sake He endured the insults of those who struck Him and spat upon Him. In His deep love, He was joyfully singing in the ear of each of us, "*Because for your sake that I have borne reproach, that shame has covered My face*" *(Ps. 69:7).* We listen to these words and answer in humility, "for my sake, You endured the injustice of the evil, the flogging and the slaps, and never turned Your face away from the shameful spitting.

The power of the Lord Christ during His passion and crucifixion appears in that He was able to destroy all those who attacked Him but He never did because of His great love for us. He was punished for our sake and gave us His peace, took upon Himself our shame and gave us His Glory.

To understand the real Power of the Lord Christ we have to ask ourselves: what could have happened if Christ had refused the humiliation and crucifixion? or had commanded the earth to swallow all who were on it, or fire to come down from Heaven and burn them? He could have done so but that would have led to our destruction due to His refusal as a Redeemer to die for us. So the Lord said, 'I'll die so that you may not die, and be mocked so that may be glorified. I came especially for your sake to sacrifice Myself and endure insults for you out of love for you and for those who insult Me'. Therefore He did not only endure injustices, but loved, forgave and prayed for the wicked interceding for them saying, "Father, forgive them, for they do not know what they do" *(Luke23:34).*

21

This is the real Power of a heart full of love, who tolerates those who trespass against Him, loves them, prays for them and sacrifices Himself for their sake.

Who of us can follow the same example and when insulted by another inferior to his rank, would forgive, defend and also promote him!

St. Peter, the Apostle, drew his sword to defend his Master when they arrested Him and he cut off the slave's ear not understanding power in its Christian spiritual concept, so the Lord asked him to put his sword back. It is good to have Holy Zeal, but violence is not our way. Our way is love. With this love the Lord healed the slave's ear and surrendered to the sinners for whose redemption He came...

Sts. John and James the Apostles also did not understand the real meaning of power and when the Lord Christ was rejected by a City, the two apostles said, *"Lord, do you want us to command fire to come down from Heaven and destroy them?"* But He turned and rebuked them*: "You do not know what manner of spirit you are of. For the Son of Man did not come to destroy men's lives but to save them." (Luke. 9:54-56).* In the same way, the Lord came willfully to the Cross, to give His life a ransom for many...

My brethren, when we stand near the Cross, we do not weep as did Mary Magdalene and the daughters of Jerusalem.. nor do we pity the Lord nor blame Him, **we stand near the Cross to glorify both the Cross and the Crucified, singing the beautiful hymn:**

THINE IS THE POWER

The Cross is our boast, as we say with St. Paul:

"But God forbid that I should boast except in the cross of our Lord Jesus Christ, by whom the world has been crucified to me, and I to the world " (Gal. 6..14).

"For the message of the Cross is foolishness to those who are perishing" but to us who are being saved, it is the power of God" (1 Cor. 1:18).

If the Cross had been a sign of weakness, it would have never been our boast and we should have never taken it as our symbol.

If the Cross had been a sign of weakness, we would have never erected it on our churches and our towers or hanged it round our necks, tattooed it on our hands and drawn it in our writings... The Cross to us is a sign of power, the power of love, sacrifice, self negligence and endurance. This is the real meaning of power...

Many said to the Lord Jesus Christ, "*If you are the Son of God, come down from the cross.. and we will believe... *" Had He accepted the challenge, it would have meant the destruction of humanity and loss of salvation. But He was too powerful to be stirred up and He remained on the Cross.

The Lord Christ was not overcome by this vain glory: save Yourself to prove You are the Son of God, to prove Your power and amaze the world by the miracle... He was not overcome by such flattery nor by the wrong concept of power... He was able to come down from the cross, but He did not so that we might be saved.

The Lord Jesus Christ never thought of Himself, but of us. He did not care about saving Himself from death, but He was concerned about saving us. by redeeming us. He did not yield to crucifixion out of weakness but out of love.

He was unselfish, for *love "does not seek its own, is not provoked" (1 Cor. 13:5)*. Had He been thinking of Himself and of how to be glorified according to the world, He would not have emptied Himself and taken the form of a slave... He did not think of Himself because He came to give Himself up for us and thus He proved to the world the power of His love and sacrifice, *"Greater love has no one than this, than to lay down one's life for his friends" (John. 15:13)*.

That is how the Lord Christ set an example of power and overcoming oneself in the Cross. It was amazing how the Lord Christ accepted all their iniquities:

" ***... as a sheep before its shearers is silent, So He opened not His mouth" (Is. 53:7).***

He was aware of the plot against Him, but He did not resist evil... He calmly said to Judas Iscariot, *"What you do, do quickly." (John. 13:27)*. The only justification for what the Lord Christ did is His desire to die for us. He had the power to destroy the Cross and those who wanted to crucify Him, but His power was greater; the power of love and sacrificing.

This Power which accompanied Him all through the journey of the cross will he the subject of our contemplation and expounding in the following pages.

He was Powerful in Accepting Death:

The Lord Christ was powerful in approaching death. People did not attack Him secretly or take Him by force. He knew that He would be arrested and knew the time, as He told the disciples, *"You know that after two days is the Passover, and the Son of Man will be delivered up to be crucified " (Matt. 26:2).* It would not be wrong to say He knew the exact hour and moment and even the place, and still He went to where they would arrest Him, and at the fixed time. And when the time He knew came, He went to wake up His disciples who were asleep at Gethsemane, Saying, *"Are you still sleeping and resting? Behold, the hour is at hand, and the Son of Man is being betrayed into the hands of sinners. Rise, let us be going. See, My betrayer is at hand " (Matt. 26:45-46).*

When the enemy approached, He went with His disciples to meet him... He wanted to give Himself up for our sake..., so He said,

"I lay down My life that I may take it again. No one takes it from Me, but I lay it down of Myself. I have power to lay it down, and I have power to take it again ... " (John 10:17-18).

The Lord Jesus Christ walked towards the enemy in power and courage, and we walk by His side saying, "Thine is the Power, the Glory, the Blessing and the Honour, forever Amen. "

The Lord had the power to put away death, but He was content in accepting it.. *"to give His life a ransom for many" (Mark. 10:45).*

He was Powerful While being Arrested:

✛ **The Lord Christ powerful when He was arrested, while the soldiers who came with sticks and swords were afraid of Him.** St. John the Beloved who followed the Lord till the Crucifixion, explained this situation saying, *"Jesus therefore, knowing all things that would come upon Him, went forward and said to them, "Whom are you seeking? They answered Him, "Jesus of Nazareth." Jesus said to them, "I am He." And Judas, who betrayed Him, also stood with them. Now when He said to them, "I am He," they drew back and fell to the ground." (John. 18:4-6).*

The Lord's enemies fell, to the ground and could not face His unarmed power which was more effective than their armed attack. Jesus could have gone away at that time, but instead he remained calm and brave.

When they stood up, once more He asked them, *"Whom do you seek? And they said, "Jesus of Nazareth". Jesus answered, "I have told you that I am He. Therefore, if you seek Me, let these go their way" (John. 18:7-9).*

That is how the Lord Jesus Christ was powerful when He was arrested. Other facing the same situation could have been shaken with fear, while with the Lord, it was the opposite: He was not afraid but those who came to arrest Him were too scared to face Him, till He presented Himself to them saying, *"I am He"*.

✣ **Another example of the power of the Lord Christ when arrested was the healing the ear of the Chief priest's slave.** *"Then Simon Peter, having a sword, drew it and struck the high priest's servant, and cut off his right ear." (John. 18:10).* But our meek Lord who does not agree to violence, turned to Peter and asked him to sheathe his sword. He refused to defend Himself or let others defend Him. He rebuked Peter saying, *"Put your sword in its place, Or do you think that I cannot now pray to My Father, and He will provide Me with more than twelve legions of angels?"(Matt.26:53).* The Lord refused to do anything to save Himself, but faced death in courage for our salvation.

As for the slave's ear, it was healed by the powerful Lord who was to be arrested, *"And He touched his ear and healed him." (Luke. 22:51).* The Lord showed mercy to His enemies even at the most critical times. **We stand beside the arrested Lord who healed the slave's ear, whispering in His holy ear, "Thwk Teti Gom", ie. Thine is the Power.**

This act of mercy put to shame the soldiers, Judas and the Chief priests. It was also a witness against them or an invitation to believe in Him later on... After being arrested, He walked among them as a King among His slaves or the Creator with His creation... He could have destroyed them all, but He wanted our salvation.

✤ **The Lord could have done what Elijah did with the Captain of the fifty who asked him to meet the king.** *"So Elijah answered and said to the Captain of fifty: If I am a man of God, let fire come down from heaven and consume you and your fifty men. And fire came down from heaven and consumed him and his fifty." (2 Kgs. 1:10)*

The Messiah could have simply done what Elijah did, but He came to die for Man. His power was in controlling Himself not to destroy them. It is the power that saved us and the courage that made Him face death without fear...

He was Strong During the Trial:

The Chief priests were afraid of the Lord, so they held His trial at night. They were confused and... *"false testimony against Jesus to put Him to death, but found none. Even though many false witnesses came forward, they found none" (Matt. 26:59-60).* They were amazed to see Him calm and silent, "So the high priest stood up and said to Him, *'And the high priest arose and said to Him, "Do You answer nothing? What is it these men testify against You? But Jesus kept silent (Matt. 26:62-63)*

Accusations did not upset the Lord Christ, neither did false witnesses. His silence was more powerful than words, it made them feel that their accusations and false witnesses were trifles. They searched for another charge and implored Him to admit that He was Christ the Son of God. *"I charge You on oath by the living God that You tell us whether You are* *the Christ, the Son of God. "* He could have kept silent but He answered powerfully, *"It is as you said. Nevertheless, I say to you hereafter you will see the Son of Man sitting at the Right Hand of the Power and coming on the clouds of heaven".* *(Matt. 62:63-64)*

He was powerful in facing Pilate as well as Caiaphas. His dignity overruled that governor who repeatedly confessed, "I find no fault in this Man." *"And indeed, having examined Him in your presence, I have found no fault in this Man concerning those things of which you accuse Him" I have found no reason for death in Him ". (Luke. 23:4,14 &21)*

No words were said to convince Pilate, but it was the Lord's silence and the power that radiated from Him. That governor tried different tricks to set Him free and when he failed he washed his hands announcing his innocence of the blood of the Lord Christ.

✛ We stand beside the Lord during the trial saying:

Thine is the Power...

He was Powerful During His Crucifixion and Death:

✛ When the Lord was on the Cross, the sun was darkened and... *"the veil of the temple was torn in two from top to bottom; and the earth quaked, and the rocks were split, and the graves were opened; and many bodies of the saints who had fallen asleep were raised" (Matt. 27:51-52).*

When the Centurion and his men, who were guarding the cross observed the earthquake they were dreadfully frightened and said, *"Truly this was the Son of God!" (Matt. 27:54)*

The Centurion became a great saint and was martyred for the name of Christ. His name is Saint Longinus and is commemorated by the church twice a year in the Sinexarium.

The sun's darkening had its effect on Athens in Greece. Due to this phenomenon, the astrologist and member of Parliament Dionosius Ariobagi believed in Christ due to the preaching of St. Paul who explained to him how the sun was darkened at the time of the crucifixion of the Lord Christ. Dionosius became the first bishop of Athens.

The Lord Christ was also powerful on the Cross when He forgave those who crucified Him and when He promised the robber on His right to be with Him in paradise that same day.

The Lord was Powerful in His Death:

✣ When His hour came... *" Jesus had cried out with a loud voice, He said, "Father, 'into Your hands I commit My spirit." (Luke. 23:46)* St. John Chrysostom chose the phrase "with a loud voice" and contemplated on the power of the Lord during His death.

How did the Lord have such a "loud voice" while dying and after He had reached a state of extreme physical weakness?

He struggled at Gethsemane... " *Then His sweat became like great drops of blood falling down to the ground.* " *(Luke. 22:45)*. He was then arrested and had to walk on foot for long distances, as He was sent for trial five times before Annas, Caiaphas, Pilate, Herod then Pilate for a second time. Added to this was the exhaustion and the unbearable pain He had when He was flogged 39 times in the most savage way, while many died or were about to die just by flogging! The crown of thorns caused Him to lose blood, besides being struck several times. Then He had to carry the Cross till He collapsed. " ***Now as they led Him away, they laid hold of a certain man, Simon a Cyrenian, who was coming from the country, and on him they laid the cross that he might bear it after Jesus.*** *" (Luke. 23:26)*.

He endured still more pain when He was nailed to the Cross till His physical power drained and His skin stuck to His bones, which conformed with the saying, "*I can count all My bones.*" *(Ps. 22:17)*

When Jesus reached the moment of death, there was no power left in Him even to whisper. How then did He cry with a loud voice?!

We stand by His side amazed at this holy moment, saying...

" THINE IS THE POWER "

✤ The Lord was powerful in His death. He defeated death by His death, battered the serpent's head and fulfilled the promise given to humanity since Eve's time... "*He shall bruise your head.* " *(Gen. 3:15)* The death of the Lord demonstrated Him as the world's Saviour.

The Lord's most powerful moment was that of His death. At that hour He reigned over humanity and restored His Kingdom from the ruler of this world. *"The Lord reigns; He has robed Himself with majesty; the Lord is clothed with strength; thus He girded Himself" (Ps.93).* He reigned on the cross.

For this reason, the prayer of the ninth hour by which we commemorate the Lord's death, is full of psalms of praise, glorifying and worship.

We stand before the Powerful Lord in His death singing:

" THINE IS THE POWER "

He was Powerful After His Death:

The first thing the Lord did when He yielded up His Spirit was laying hold of the devil and binding him for a thousand years. The Lord also... *"descended into the lower parts of the earth. " (Eph. 4:9)* He announced the good news to the dead and led them, with the robber who was on His right, to Paradise.

It was the Lord's death that opened the gate of Paradise after being locked for thousands of years, since Adam and Eve's fall.

The One they thought dead in the sealed tomb was able to open the gate to Paradise and lead all who died on hope in His procession of victory.

One of the beautiful stories about the Lord after His death is that Nicodemus said, "Holy God, Holy Mighty, Holy Immortal..." from which the well known Trisagion is taken.

We stand by the side of the holy tomb, saying to the Lord in His death...

" THINE IS THE POWER "

✣ The Lord was powerful in His Resurrection: powerful when He left the sealed tomb and conquered death.

The Lord Hid His Power From the Devil:

One of the main reasons that make people think that the Lord Christ was weak is that He used to hide His power.

It was an act of humility that confused the devil and made him wonder, 'Is that really Jesus Christ!' 'He or not He!'.

It was for the best not to let the devil know the truth about the Lord Jesus Christ, as he could have done his utmost to cripple the mission of redemption for the devil never wanted the world to be saved.

The following examples illustrate the devil's confusion because of the Lord hiding His power:

✣ The devil knew that the Lord Christ would be born from a virgin as Isaiah the Prophet said clearly..." "*Behold the virgin shall conceive and bear a Son, and shall call His name Emmanuel*" *(Is. 7:14)* He also described the qualities of this

Son, *"For unto Us a Child is born, unto Us a Son is given and the government will be upon His shoulder: and His name will be called Wonderful, Counsellor, Mighty God, Everlasting Father, Prince of Peace. " (Is. 9:6).*

The devil heard a confirmation of this prophecy when the angel appeared to Joseph and said *"Behold! The virgin shall be with child and bear a son, and they shall call His name Emmanuel"* *(Matt. 1:22-23)*

It was also confirmed in the angel's annunciation to Virgin Mary that... *"The Holy Spirit will come upon you, and the power of the Highest will overshadow you; therefore, also, that Holy One who is to be born will be called the Son of God" (Luke. 1:35).* And it happened that the Virgin Mary did conceive and the devil witnessed what happened when Mary visited Elizabeth, " when Elizabeth heard the greeting of Mary, that the babe leaped in her womb; and *Elizabeth was filled with the Holy Spirit. Then she spoke out with a loud voice and said, but why is this granted to me, that the mother of my Lord should come to me?" (Luke. 1:43).*

The devil then said within himself that this was certainly the Son of God.

But when the Incarnated God was born in a manger, the devil was very confused.

How could that happen! It is hard to believe that this poor, homeless baby, who is surrounded by animals, is the Son of God. It cannot be He, without the whole world celebrating His coming with ceremonies, guarded by angels and heavenly lights to announce His arrival and the heaven and earth shaking before Him.

The devil was confused as he had no idea about the meaning of humbleness or self humiliation; otherwise he would not have become a devil...

✣ **The devil also heard what the angel announced to, the shepherds**, "*Do not be afraid, for behold, I bring you good tidings of great joy which will be to all people. For there is born to you this day in the city of David a Saviour, who is Christ the Lord. And this will be the sign to you: You will find a Babe wrapped in swaddling cloths, lying in a manger* " *(Luke. 2:10-12)*

And the devil said within himself, 'that is certainly He'. This was confirmed by the multitude of heavenly host, praising God and saying, "*Glory to God in the highest and on earth peace, good will toward men.* " *(Luke. 2:14)* If peace was to return to earth, then it should be the Lord Christ, the Saviour. This was also ascertained by the testimony of the wise men, the fulfilment of the prophecy about the baby of Bethlehem, the disturbance of King Herod because of the Child's birth and worship of the wise men to the Child. *(Matt. 2:1-11)*.

However, the devil later on suspected the matter when he saw that great Saviour who was praised by the angels and worshipped by the wise men and who caused Herod to tremble, that great Saviour fly in fear to Egypt. He thought: Is it possible that God escapes from the face of Man? Where is His power, His Kingdom and awe. It cannot be He...

✣ But the devil then saw that when that Child entered Egypt, many of its idols fell and were broken. He knew that that fulfilled the prophecy of Isaiah which said, *"Behold, the Lord is riding on a swift cloud and comes to Egypt; the idols of Egypt will totter at His presence and the heart of the Egyptians will melt in its midst. " (Is. 19:1).* And the devil said within himself, "No doubt, He is the Saviour, the Son of God".

Once more the devil became in doubt when he realised that the Child returned only after the death of those who were seeking His life. He also saw that, *"But when he heard that Archelaus was reigning over Judea instead of his father Herod, he was afraid to go there. And being warned by God in a dream, he turned aside into the region of Galilee. And he came and dwelt in a city called Nazareth " (Matt. 2:22,23).* What a confusing situation! *"Can anything good come out of Nazareth " (John. 1:46).* 'No, it cannot be He!' said the devil.

✣ The devil remained in his doubts till the Child was twelve years of age and saw Him sitting among the elderly teachers and all who listened to Him were amazed at His understanding. The devil heard Jesus answering Mary and Joseph, *"Did you not know that I must be about My Father's business ". (Luke. 2:49).* The devil then said within himself, 'It must be He. Who else will have such wisdom and talk about His Father's business!'.

When the boy submitted himself to Mary and Joseph, the devil started to doubt again. How would He yield to them while heaven and earth must submit to Him. It cannot be He! What increased his doubts was seeing Jesus Christ living for 18 years, (till He was 30 years old), as a simple carpenter with no fame at all. The Lord would not waste the prime of His life in such a way. It cannot be He.

The devil then heard John the Baptist who testified for Christ saying, "...*but there is One who stands among you, whom you do not recognise, the One who will come after me and whose sandal-strings I am unworthy to untie.*"

He pointed out to Christ and said, "Behold! The Lamb of God who takes away the sin of the world!" *(John. 1:26-29). "There comes One after me who is mightier than I. I indeed baptised you with water, but He will baptise you with the Holy Spirit." (Mark. 1:7,8).*And the devil said; it must be He

The devil was mostly amazed when he saw that great Lord who John the Baptist said he was not worthy to stoop down and untie the thong of His sandals and was supposed to take away the sins of the world and baptise with the Holy spirit, that great Lord come to John to be baptised like everyone else.

The devil expected Christ to baptise John and start His mission; that is what dignity means. But he saw exactly the opposite happen. He heard Christ saying to John, "*Let it be so now*". And John did baptise Christ. It was too much for the devil to understand this humility and he said in his heart, 'It is not He!'

✜ During the baptism, a remarkable sign was given to prove that it was He. The devil saw the heavens parted and the Spirit, like a dove, coming down upon Christ. There also came a voice from heaven, "*You are My beloved Son, in whom I am well pleased" (Mark. 1:10-11).* There was no doubt in that clear testimony of the Father. It is certainly He.

The devil then returned to his doubts when he saw that He, to whom the Father and the Holy Spirit gave testimony during the baptism, was lying exhausted on the mountain, hungry after fasting.

How would He be hungry while having the power to turn the stones into bread to eat. Surely it was not He.

✧ The devil was able to take Him and set Him on the pinnacle of the temple, then to a high mountain. *(Matt. 4:5-8).* The devil then was so certain that it could not be the Son of God, and dared to say to Him, *"All these things I will give You if You will fall down and worship me" (Matt. 4:9).* But his fear returned when the Lord rebuked him saying, *"Begone, Satan!... Then the devil left Him, and behold, angels came and ministered to Him." (Matt. 4:11).*

✧ The devil's fear increased and began to think that it was He when he saw Him work miracles nobody else worked before. But he found that the Lord hid some of those miracles behind His prayers. Other miracles He worked on the Sabbath, which led to the anger of the Pharisees and scribes. The devil, seeing the Lord living with no title, no position no residence, surrounded by weak people said to himself, 'No, it is not He!'

✧ The devil then heard Christ say to Nicodemus, *"No one has ascended to heaven but He who came down from heaven, that is, the Son of Man who is in heaven ". (John. 3:13).* And the devil said: could it be He?! But how could He be in heaven while being on earth with Nicodemus!

If He is to be found everywhere, then He must be God. It is also confirmed by the phrase, *"descended from heaven"*. Besides, he heard the Lord saying, *"For God so loved the world that He gave His only begotten Son, that whoever believes in Him should not perish but have everlasting life." (John. 3:16)*.

✣ These words nearly convinced the devil, whose doubts returned to him because of the expression Son of Man" which the Lord often used. But why does He say that *"the Son of Man must be lifted up so that whoever believes in Him may not perish but have everlasting life" (John.3:14-17)*.

✣ The numerous miracles of the lord Christ proved His divinity, and His power over evil spirits forced them to admit it. *"And demons also came out of many, crying out and saying, "You are the Christ, the Son of God! He rebuked them". (Luke. 4:41)*. The devil's suspicions started again when he found that the Lord was tired of walking, sitting by a well or asking a woman for a drink!!

✣ **When the Lord rebuked the sea and waves, the devil said, 'It is He, But when He was asleep in the ship, he wondered how could it be and it says in the Psalm,** "He will neither slumber nor sleep"!!

✣ Some people were just as confused as the devil himself. *"Some say John the Baptist, some Elijah, and others Jeremiah or one of the prophets." (Matt. 16:14)*. The Lord asked His disciples, *"But you, who do you say I am?"* Simon Peter answered, "*You are Christ, the Son of the Living God*" *and the Lord answered him, "Blessed are you, Simon Bar-Jonah, for flesh and blood has not revealed this to you, but My Father who is in heaven." (Matt. 16:17).*

The devil heard this clear, unquestionable confession and said to himself, 'No doubt it is He.'

The devil's confusion started again when he heard the Lord tell His disciples that He must go to Jerusalem to suffer, die and on the third day rise. And the devil could not understand how would the Son of God suffer and die. It must be His way of saving Man, then He should be stopped. So the devil put words on Peter's mouth to say to his Lord "*God forbid, Lord! This shall never happen to You!*" But turning around, the Lord said to Peter, "*Get behind Me, Satan! You are an offence to Me, for you are not mindful of the things of God, but the things of men.*" *(Matt. 16:22)*

✣ The devil then thought it might be He when the Lord left to Jerusalem where He was received as a great king, the awaited Messiah and even the children praised Him in fulfilment of the Psalm. "*Out of the mouth of babes and nursing infants You have ordained strength...*" *(Ps. 8:2),* and in His respectfulness cleansed the temple. But his doubts returned when the Lord retired to Bethany...

✣ The Lord started to destroy the devil's kingdom, revealing to the people the hypocrisy of the scribes and Pharisees saying, "*Woe to you, scribes and, Pharisees. hypocrites...* " *(Matt. 23:1-3).* He did away also with the Levitical priesthood by telling the parable of the vineyard and the wicked tenants. *(Luke. 20: 9-19)*.

The Lord put to shame also the Pharisees, Sadducces and the Herodians that *"no one dared question Him " (Mark. 12:34)*. Thereupon the devil began to get ready to arrest the Lord and so the plot developed on Wednesday...

✢ **The devil saw the Lord washing the disciples' feet on Thursday and He got encouraged saying in his heart it was not the Lord; for how would the Lord wash the feet of men?! And so the devil got inside Judas after the piece of bread and made him carry out the plot.** *(John13:2)*....

✢ When the devil heard the Lord's last talk with the disciples and that He would send them the Holy Spirit, he thought it must be He; for who else could send God's Holy spirit except God Himself!

✢ The devil then hearing the Lord's long prayer to the Father, asking for the disciples, *"that they may be one as We are." (John. 17:11).” as You, Father, are in Me, and I in You" (John. 17:21), "Keep through Your name those... that they may be one as We are"*. the devil trembled and said 'it must be He? He remembered the Lord's words *before "I and My father are One". (John. 10:30),* and His words to Philip, *"He who has seen Me has seen the Father,- So how can you say, 'Show us the father? 'Do you not believe that I am in the Father and the Father in Me?" (John 14:8-10),* and the devil was filled with fear and said, 'It must be He?'..

But soon the devil saw the Lord in His agony on the Mount of Olives, asking the Father if He would remove that cup from Him, and exclaimed how would the One who said, *"I and the Father are One"*, **be in such agony, till** *"His sweat fell to the ground like great drops of blood"* *(Luke 22:44)!*And the devil was assured and said, 'No, it is not He." The soldiers then came to arrest Him...

✧ The devil saw the soldiers who came armed with swords, weapons and sticks to arrest the Lord Christ fall to the ground and not able to face His overwhelming reverence, though He was unarmed, and the devil became puzzled. He saw the Lord heal the car of the slave when Peter severed it with his sword, and the devil said 'Certainly, it is He'. Who else would have such courage and reverence. Who else would have such love towards His enemies and have such miraculous power... But soon the devil saw the Lord walking with them as a lamb to the slaughter, not opening His mouth. And the devil Was assured again and said, 'No is not He...'

✧ Then the Lord was put to trial by the chief priests, and the devil listened carefully. He was trying to find an answer to the question he had in mind since the temptation on the mount. The question this time came from the chief priest who asked the Lord, *"Are You Christ, the Son of God?"* And the Lord said to him, *"Nevertheless, I say to you, hereafter you will see the Son of Man sitting at the right hand of the Power, and coming on the clouds of heaven."* *(Matt26:64)*.

The devil heard this clear confession and wondered if it was He who has said many times before, would come upon the clouds of heaven! But the devil's doubts returned when he

saw the Lord despised and forsaken by the people who mocked and spitefully treated Him, and He opened not His mouth. He offered His back to be flogged and His cheek to be slapped, and did not turn His face away from the humility of spit...

He saw the Lord fall with exhaustion under the Cross, and Simon Cyrene carry it for Him. The devil then said, 'No, it is impossible to be He? Dignity and power according to the devil meant false glory. So he said to himself 'It cannot be He'. And the devil shouted on the mouth of the public, "*Crucify Him, Crucify Him*"... But the echo of the Lord's words remained, "*I lay down My life... I voluntarily lay it down and I have authority to take it up again...* "

✛ **The Lord was lifted on the Cross and the devil continued tormented with doubt. The Lord hid his power and the devil continued asking the old question, "*...Save Yourself! If You are the Son of God, come down from the cross.*" (Matt. 27:40).**

The Lord's first words while on the Cross started with, "Father"..."*Father, forgive them..*" The word "Father" disturbed the devil, and he asked himself, 'Could it be He?' And by putting words on the mouth of the robber on the left, he asked "*If You are the Christ, save Yourself and us*" (Luke23:39).

✛ The Lord said to the robber on His right hand, "*Truly I say to you, today you will be with Me in Paradise*" (Luke. 23:42). And the devil was shaken with fear. What is it that He says?! Does not He know that Paradise have been locked five thousand years... "*And at the east of the garden of Eden He placed the Cherubim, and a flaming sword which turned every way, to guard the way to the tree of life.* " (Gen. 3:24). How would Paradise be then open? And how would the Crucified enter it with the other robber?! Could it be the Christ, by whose Crucifixion the world will be saved?! If that happened, it would be a catastrophe befalling Satan's kingdom and all that he achieved since Adam...

✛ On the sixth hour, there was darkness over earth, the veil of the temple was torn in two, the earth shook, the rocks were split and tombs were opened, and the devil's terror increased and he said, 'It is He, no doubt, Christ the Saviour.'

✛ **But in spite of the shaking of the earth and darkness, the devil beard the Lord say, "My God, My God, why have You forsaken Me? "., then say, "I am Thirsty "., And the devil calmed down and said, 'It is not He'.**

The devil waited for the death of the Lord Christ to get hold of His soul, as he did with other human beings, and bring Him down to Hade. But the devil was taken by surprise when the Lord cried with a loud voice, *"Father, into Your hands I entrust My spirit"*.

The devil was astonished to hear the Crucified-still saying "Father". Could He be truly the Son of God? What was the meaning of that loud voice? How did He get that strength? And the devil said to himself, 'How would He entrust His spirit into God's hands. It has to be in my hands'.

But when the devil progressed to take the soul of the Lord while still in fear and doubt, the Lord held him with the power of His divinity and bound him for a thousand years.

AND THE GLORY
ⲚⲈⲙ ⲠⲓⲰⲞⲨ

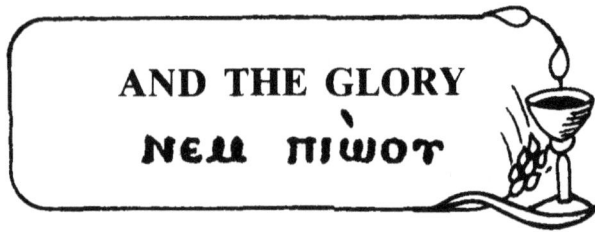

During the Passion Week, we see the Lord Christ as described by the prophet *"... He is despised and rejected by men ... and we esteemed Him not. " (Is. 53:3).* We look at Him despised for our sake and follow Him, singing this immortal hymn, *"Thine is the Power, the Glory, the Blessing and the Honour, forever Amen, Emmanuel our God and King".*

Despised and Rejected by Men!!

In fact, the Lord did not abandon His glory during the Passion week only, but He also sacrificed His dignity for our sake all the time.

He became without Honour in His own country. They reproached Him saying, *"Is this not the carpenter's son?"* *(Matt. 13:55).* For us He endured shame, insults and reproach...

Being humble, the Lord sat with tax-collectors and sinners, but they called Him a gluttonous and a winebibber. For His love which appeared in healing the sick, they accused Him of breaking the Sabbath, and, for His concern to teach us to go into the depth instead of abiding by the letter, they said He violated the Law. We see Him abused for our sake and we follow Him with the same hymn, "Thine is the Power and Glory...

We know, Lord, why they insulted You. They did that because You were not like them and Your humility exposed them.

You did not behave like them, for, *"But all their works they do to be seen by men. They make their phylacteries broad and enlarge the borders of their garments. They love the best places at feasts, the best seats in the synagogues, greetings in the marketplaces, and to be called by men, 'Rabbi, Rabbi."* *(Matt. 23:5- 7).* But You lived modest and meek, mixing with the low and despised, eating with sinners and tax-collectors. You let the woman who was a sinner touch You, the Samaritan woman argue with You, and the children come to You. You walked in poverty, with no title, no money and nowhere to lean on Your head.

They refused to glorify You, Lord, for You despised their glory and said, "*I do not receive Glory from men.* " (John. 5:41). So You refused the kingdom and majesty. But we, aware of Your Real Majesty, address You saying, "Thine is the Power, and the Glory..."

Their despise did not decrease Your glory at all. They sold You for the price of a slave *"Thirty pieces of silver"* and mockingly, they put a purple robe on You and a crown of thorns upon Your Head. As for us, we follow You in Your passion saying," *"Thine is the Power, the Glory, the Blessing and the Honour, forever Amen"*...

You Are Our Glorified God:

They despised You, because You took upon You the form of a servant, but we glorify You, as we know who You are...

You are equal to the Father as You said, *"All Yours are Mine" (John. 17:10).* And You are the Only Begotten son, who is in the bosom of the Father, since the beginning *(John. 1:18),* *"Who being the brightness of His Glory and the express image of His person" (Heb. 1:3). Yes Lord, we glorify You for the glory which " You had with Your Father before the world was."* *(John 17:5),* and because all authority in heaven and earth had been given to You. *(Matt. 28:18).*

You had been glorified before we came into being, and for You *"every knee should bow, of those in heaven, and of those on earth, and of those under the earth " (Phil. 2:10).*

Before we began to glorify You, You were and still are glorified by the Angels and Archangels... [Before whom stand thousands of thousands and ten thousand of the heavenly hosts ministering to You... and carry out Your word, our Master.]

You had been also glorified before the Angels or anything else existed, when You alone existed. You do not need any creature to glorify You, for You are glorified in Your Nature, Your attributes, and Your Divinity. You need no one to glorify You and as You said, *"I am the Alpha and the Omega, the Beginning and the End, the First and the Last." (Rev. 22:13).*

When we glorify You, Lord, we do not add something new to You, for even in Your self-humiliation, many events showed Your glory...

You were glorified on Your birth by the angels who brought the good tidings to the shepherds, and by the three wise men who brought you gifts that suited Your glory and worshipped You. You were glorified when the idols of Egypt fell on Your visit while still a child. *(Is. 19:1)*. John the Baptist glorified You saying, "..."*There comes One after me who is mightier than I, whose sandal strap I am not worthy to stoop down and loose.* " *(Mark 1: 7,8)*.

Your glory was shown during the Baptism, when the Holy Spirit descended on You like a dove, and a voice from heaven said, "*You are My beloved Son; in You I am well pleased.*"*(Luke 3:22)*.

Your glory was also shown on the Mount of transfiguration, when Your face shone like the sun and Your garments became white as light, and God's voice from a cloud said, "*This is My beloved Son, in whom I am well pleased. Hear Him!* " *(Matt. 17:2-5)*.

You showed Your glory, Lord, in numerous miracles, even the devils could not help but bear witness. And when You were tempted by Satan on the mountain, You showed Your glory... You rebuked the devil and he was gone, then the angels came and ministered to You. *(Mark 1:13)*.

Your glory was shown through the Revelation to St. John the Visionary, who saw You in the midst of golden

lampstands. Your face shone as when the sunshines in its full strength, Your eyes were like a flame of fire, and Your voice like the sound of many waters... When St. John saw You, he fell at Your feet as dead. *(Rev. 1:13-17)*.

In Your second coming, You will also come in Your Glory, on clouds of heaven, as it is said, *"When the Son of Man comes in His glory, and all the holy angels with Him, then He will sit on the throne of His glory " (Matt. 25:31)*. *"Clouds and darkness surround Him, Righteousness and Justice are the foundation of His throne... His lightning illumine the world.. The mountains melt like wax before the Lord. " (Ps. 97..2-5)*.

We also Glorify You:

When glorifying You, our mouths are sanctified, but that does not add anything to You. When we glorify You, Lord, we do not give you glory, but rather admit Yours. You are like the sun; it shines with or without our acknowledgment. What we say does not add to its light; it illuminates by itself...

We do not glorify You only in Your second coming, when Your glory will be obvious, but we glorify You in the depth of Your passion. We follow You, step by step proclaiming, "Thine is the Power and Glory... Emmanuel our God and King". We Glorify You with the beautiful hymn... the magnificent, immortal melody which is incomparable in the world of music, in which we say, *"Your throne, O God, is forever and ever; A sceptre of righteousness is the sceptre of Your kingdom." (Ps. 45:6)*.

By glorifying You, Christ, we protest against the deeds of those who plotted and crucified You. We protest against what the ungrateful human beings did to You, and see Your true glory in the Cross You endured for our sake. By glorifying You in Your crucifixion, we have pride in the glory of the Cross, taking it as a life and support for us in our ministry. We even sing with St. Paul, "*I have been crucified with Christ; it is no longer I who live, but Christ lives in me* ". *(Gal. 2:20).*

With this beautiful hymn we glorify the Lord at the end of the prayers of the Good Friday, after He paid His blood a price for the world's salvation, and began to reign on a tree. We sing to Him, "*Your Throne, 0 God, is for ever and ever...* " With the same hymn, we also glorify Him on Tuesday of the Passion week, the day on which He announced to the disciples the time of His crucifixion, "*You know that after two days is the Passover, and the Son of Man will be delivered up to be crucified.* " *(Matt. 26:2).* And with the same beautiful tune we glorify the Lord with another hymn ie. **ⲀⲦⲞⲚⲞⲚ** (Avchenon)*.

We glorify You, Lord, in Your crucifixion not only in Your miracles...

----

* This hymn is part of (Ps. 55) usually sung with the same tune of "Your throne 0 God" on Wednesday night of the Passion Week.

AND THE BLESSING
ⲚⲈⲙ ⲡⲓⲥⲙⲟⲧ

We follow our Lord Jesus Christ in the Crucifixion, whispering in His ear, "Thine is The Blessing" as the Holy Bible says, " *Cursed is everyone who hangs on a tree.* " *(Gal. 3:13).*

For this reason, a criminal put to death in that way had to be buried on the same day and not remain all night hanged on the tree, lest he should defile the land, as the hanged is accursed by God. *(Dent. 21:22-23).* And so the Lord took away the curse of the Law on our behalf and became accursed for our sake.

But we know that He is holy, without sin, and the curse He took away was ours; the wages of our sins according to the Law. *(Dent. 28:27).* He is not a sinner, certainly not, but He takes away the sins of others, of the whole world. We therefore, follow Him regretting for what we made Him carry, saying to Him from the depths of our hearts, *"Thine is the Power, the Glory, the Blessing... Emmanuel our God and King"*...

For this curse, they crucified Him outside the camp,- so that He would not defile it, and we follow Him in His Passion Week, as *St. Paul said, "Accordingly, let us go forth to Him outside the camp, bearing His reproach" (Heb. 13:13).*

We bear His reproach, as said about the Prophet Moses, *"esteeming the reproach of Christ greater riches than the treasures in Egypt; for he looked to the reward. " (Heb. 11:26).*

For this reason the Church remains outside the camp, away from the altar, away from the sanctuary, away from the first Chancel, the Chancel of Saints, remembering our sins that took us outside the camp like Adam when sent forth from the garden of Eden. We follow the Lord outside the Camp saying, "You are righteous, we are evil, we deserve the curse and banishment, but You, Thine is the Blessing forever Amen, my Lord Jesus Christ, the Good Saviour.

While the Jews see in the Cross of the Lord Christ a symbol of shame and humiliation, we say to Him: To You and to Your cross is the blessing. With Your Cross we are blessed in everything. The priests, with the sign of the Cross, bless the Congregation, and with the sign of the Cross, the consecration and sanctification are completed.

With the sign of the Cross in the baptistery, we obtain the blessing of the new birth and each member of our body is blessed and sanctified with the sign of the Cross in the sacrament of the Holy Chrism. Besides, all the Holy sacraments of Eucharist, Priesthood and the other sacraments of the Church are completed with the sign of the Cross by which we obtain grace, blessing and gifts. So, we cry out from all our hearts, "Thine is the Blessing........

We cross our food before we start eating and ourselves before we go to sleep and with this sign we become blessed in everything. We look at the blessings of the Cross and say to the

Lord in His passion, "Thine is the Blessing, forever Amen, Emmanuel our God and King".

Thine, 0 Lord, is the blessing that we lost since the fall of Adam, and of which we dreamt till this day, waiting for You to grant to us; You, by whom all the nations of the world are blessed.

When Man was created, God blessed him, and when he fell, a curse came unto earth, as God said to Adam, *"Cursed is the ground because of you" (Gen. 3:17).* Then the curse spread among human being themselves, so God cursed Cain *(Gen. 4:11),* then Canaan and his descendants too.

The curse extended and reached every sinner, as it was said in the Law, *"If you will not obey the voice of the Lord Your God or be careful in following all His commandments and His statutes which I command you this day, then all these curses shall come upon and overtake you... The Lord will send you curses, confusion and frustration in all that you undertake to do, until you are a-destroyed and perish quickly" (Dent. 28:15-20).*

Amidst the curses of the Law, mankind dreamt of God fulfilling His promise to Abraham, ... *"In your seed all the nations of the earth shall be blessed. " (Gen. 22:18).*

Mankind waited for Your coming, Lord, then You came our loving, kind Lord to take away the curse of the Law and in You all nations be blessed. We stand by Your side while on the Cross, trusting Your promise to Abraham.

We look at You, Lord, while You dip hyssop in Your Holy Blood and sprinkle us to become clean. We sing for Your Glory and Holiness: "Thine is the Blessing, forever Amen".

Thine is the Blessing:

Thine is the blessing that You gave to the world in whom are blessed by all nations and generations. But for this blessing of Yours, the whole world would perish in its sins.

Thine is the blessing as we say to You in the Holy Mass "You blessed my nature in You". Thine is the unlimited blessing by which the whole world are blessed...

Thine is the blessing You gave us, the nation who were called uncircumcised, "*that at that time you were without Christ, being aliens from the commonwealth of Israel and strangers from the covenants of promise, having no hope and without God in the world.*" (Eph. 2:12). With Your blessings, Lord we "*...you are no longer strangers and foreigners, but fellow citizens with the saints and members of the household of God.*" (Eph. 2:19).

Thine is the blessing because You are Holy, so, on the day of Your crucifixion, we sing this hymn saying, "Holy God, Holy Mighty, Holy Immortal, who was crucified for us, have mercy upon us..." As we sing the hymn of Your Holiness, we clear You from all accusations.

When we sing the "**AGIOS**" hymn i.e. "The Trisagion" with a sad tune, our sorrow is not for You, but for those who led You to the Cross as a sinner and charged You with the improper.

But You the Holy, born of the Holy Spirit, the only Holy One, Thine is the blessing forever Amen.

You first gave You. blessing to the criminal on Your right, when You brought him with You to Paradise. With this blessing, You blessed the foolish of the world and disgraced the wise, You blessed the weak porcelain vessels that carried Your Holy Name...

Who ever thought those weak fishermen would become in Your hands, like the five loaves and fill up the whole world, "*...their line has gone out through all the earth, and their words to the end of the world. " (Ps. 19..4).* Who ever thought this scared group hiding in the upper room would go and face emperors, philosophies and religions, and fill the whole world... It is Your blessing that was given to our mother Rebekah, when You said to her, "*Our sister, may you become The mother of thousands of ten thousands; And may your descendants possess The gates of those who hate them. " (Gen. 24:60).*

Indeed Lord, Thine is the Power...

The sin hid the blessing, so, when the sin was taken away from us, the blessing returned. You restored Man to his first rank, as You said to him in compassion, "*I will make you a great nation; I will bless you And make your name great; And you shall be a blessing." (Gen. 12:2).* We ask You to keep your blessing on us, with all its grace and abundance... Let the blessing we heard on the sixth day return to us, when You said. "*Be fruitful and multiply, and fill the earth and subdue it. " (Gen. 1:28).*

As for me, my soul magnifies the Lord and all that is within me blesses His Holy Name:

BLESS THE LORD, 0 MY SOUL,
AND ALL THAT IS WITHIN ME,
BLESS HIS HOLY NAME!
BLESS THE LORD, 0 MY SOUL;
AND FORGET NOT ALL HIS BENEFITS".
(Ps. 103:1-2)

AND THE HONOR

ⲚⲈⲙ ⲡⲓⲁⲙⲁϩⲓ

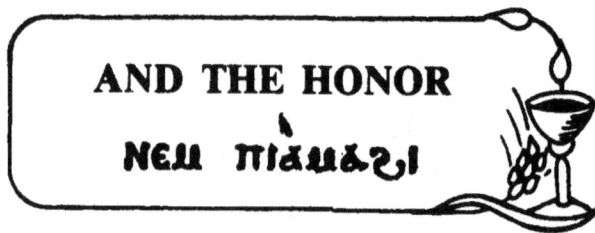

Thine is the Honour, as You are *"Lord of Lords and King of Kings" (Rev. 17:14).*

And though You refused the worldly reign, You reign over the hearts and Your Kingdom is within us. Even those who did not give You their hearts feared you.

Thine is the Honour, as You have reverence, respect and awe...

You can humble Yourself as You wish, or neglect Yourself in humility, but that does not lessen Your glory and reverence.

Many times Your self-humiliation gave a chance to your enemies to stone You or hurt You, but... passing through the midst of them You went away and no one could do You harm. *(Luke. 4:30).*

They failed to arrest You till the hour came, the hour that You fixed to give up Yourself, with Your own will. They were all afraid to face You and when they asked, they could not keep their argument. You and when they asked, they could not keep their argument. You were mighty in Your words with them, even as a Young Boy. They listened to You and were astonished and amazed...

Even the devil used to feel deep inside that You are mighty and unconquerable. Your humility allowed him to approach You, but Your awe overcame him when You rebuked him. He escaped from You, and could not finish his talk. His temptation came to an end.

Lord, You have been mighty, respected and feared all Your life. The story of the Cross is just a reaction of the fear of Your enemies. They felt You are more powerful and closer to the hearts than them. You were more convincing with people, so they feared for their authority.

We stand by the side of Your Cross, Lord, and say, in spite of these insults and sufferings, "Thine is the Honour forever Amen, Emmanuel our God and King".

www.ingramcontent.com/pod-product-compliance
Lightning Source LLC
Chambersburg PA
CBHW060611030426
42337CB00018B/3037